Ffestiniog Railway
Recollections

© John Stretton 2011

Photos: © as credited

Characters © Ken Kimberley, author of *Oi Jimmy Knacker*, *Heavo Heavo Lash Up & Stow* and *Knock Down Ginger* (published by Silver Link)

First published in 2011

ISBN 978 1 85794 372 6

British Library Cataloguing in Publication Data
A catalogue record for this book is available from the British Library
Printed and bound in the Czech Republic
Silver Link Publishing Ltd
The Trundle
Ringstead Road
Great Addington
Kettering
Northants NN14 4BW

Tel/Fax: 01536 330588
email: sales@nostalgiacollection.com
Website: www.nostalgiacollection.com

Contents

Acknowledgments

As with projects of any size and/or complexity, there are many people 'behind the scenes' who give of their time, expertise, advice, etc willingly but often receive little in the way of thanks in return. The same is true with numerous individuals within the Ffestiniog family who have helped me with this and my previous books on both the FR and WHR.

This latest may be smaller in size than the usual books on the railway but it is no narrower in scope and all involved have given of their time and expertise freely and without complaint. They are hereby thanked, but special mention should be made, for their individual assistance, to (in no special order): Andy Savage, for proofreading the text; Howard Wilson, for allowing access to his father-in-law's images; Peter Arnold for his images; Clare Britton; John Wooden; Peter Rowlands; and Peter Townsend, Will Adams and David Walshaw. Without their support and input the book would not have happened!

all manner of business influences, not least in the 21st century the demands of Health & Safety. This does not prevent the real pleasure and enjoyment on offer to the visiting public – young and old – as can be witnessed here, with *Merddin Emrys* being the centre of attention as it passes the old engine shed at Boston Lodge on 2 May 1993 with the 1500 Blaenau Ffestiniog-Porthmadog down train. *MJS*

Title page **BOSTON LODGE:** Over the years the Ffestiniog Railway has either been advertised or referred to in print as a 'Toy Railway'. This has stemmed, to some degree, from it being smaller than what is now regarded as the 'Standard Gauge', ie 4ft 8½in between the rails. However, the FR is far from being a toy, operating in every way as a professional and commercial organisation, subject to

Right **MINFFORDD:** While there are a number of paid staff on the railway, it is true to say that it could not function at the level now required without volunteer input. Back in 1963 the mode of dress is different from what would be seen today, but the happy, smiling faces are the same, as two stalwart supporters – Norman Pearce, the S&T Engineer, and Ron Lester, PW foreman but also covering the Station Master role – stand at Minffordd on AGM day, recorded for posterity. *Howard Wilson collection*

Introduction

I made my first visit to the Festiniog Railway (as it was then spelled) on 16 August 1966. On holiday in Colwyn Bay with my parents and my then girlfriend, she and I had a day away from 'the oldies' and landed up at Tan y Bwlch, which at that time was the northern terminus of the railway. Memory is hugely selective and how we arrived there from Colwyn Bay is now a complete blank. I cannot recall researching the route in advance or the bus services to take us there, or how we made our way from Porthmadog to Bangor, from where we caught a train back to Colwyn Bay! I vaguely remember standing on Colwyn Bay station early in the day, but whether the rest of the journey was by way of Llandudno Junction and Blaenau Ffestiniog, I have no idea. As I and Gill, my girlfriend, split the following year, I cannot now ask her! Suffice to say that we ventured to the FR station at Tan y Bwlch and I was captivated by what I saw.

I suppose I must have read something about the railway – probably in *Trains Illustrated,* which was my favourite at the time – but I had no idea what was in store. The station layout was then open, unfenced and very relaxed. Perhaps the hot day helped, but it all felt laid-back and unhurried. *Linda* simmered at the head of its train, waiting to run to Porthmadog, and I was fascinated by its design, being able to get 'up close and personal' and, being smaller than the standard gauge to which I was used, able to inspect more of it. We enjoyed our trip down the line and watching *Linda* being serviced in Harbour station.

Thus was a love affair born that is still as powerful today – with the railway, if not with Gill!

My next visit was in July 1979, with wife and two small children in tow, an experience repeated 12 months later. Something of my fascination and enthusiasm for the railway must have permeated their subconscious during these two years, as just over a decade later my daughter, then aged 13, became a volunteer on the railway, to be followed by my wife – especially as sign-writer – not long after. They are both still volunteers on occasions, two decades later.

I have thoroughly enjoyed my exposure to and experiences of the railway since that first time in 1966 and, likewise, I have derived a huge amount of pleasure in putting together this small collection of 'recollections'. I have taken us on an imagined journey from Porthmadog to Blaenau Ffestiniog, using views from 1960 to the present day. They show what has captivated the enthusiasts both in the past and today, and I trust that the reader will derive an equal amount of pleasure from viewing the scenes, and that it will encourage one and all to visit the railway and venture out to see just what there is on offer. You will not be disappointed!

Left **PORTHMADOG:** First I must claim the reader's forbearance, as the onlookers in the foreground are sharp but, sadly, the locomotive and train are in soft focus. However, there are relatively few colour portraits of *Merddin Emrys* in this 'incomplete' square-tanked state. Having just run into the Harbour station confines, it is seen being coupled to its 'mixed' train before its journey up the line to Tan y Bwlch in 1962, a year after entering service. *Peter Arnold*

PORTHMADOG

Below **PORTHMADOG:** Forward some six years from the last photograph, and we have a clearer view of the original layout of Harbour station – with the addition of the white fencing – as the 'old' *Earl of Merioneth* looks magnificent in its attractive green livery with red and black lining, before its departure on a bright spring day in April 1968. Named *Livingston Thompson* by the original FR Company – and *Taliesin* from the 1930s to 1961 – it reverted to its original persona after withdrawal in 1971. It is now ensconced in the National Railway Museum in York. Note the original spelling of the town name, before it was 'Welshified'. *Dennis Weaver, MJS collection*

Above **PORTHMADOG:** As seasons passed, passenger numbers increased and each new year saw more people wishing to enjoy a ride. Train lengths increased, with the railway having to consequently provide extra coaching stock and suitable motive power. The railway's iconic 'double-engines' came into their own, with their greater power output, and 1879-vintage *Merddin Emrys* was in constant use. Approaching its centenary, it steams into Harbour station with its train from Dduallt in 1973. Note the white line along the platform edge and the late-lamented Britannia Foundry in the background, which, out of use from 1965, was demolished in the late 1970s. *Jon Marsh*

FFESTINIOG RAILWAY

| Bl Ffestiniog to PENRHYN | THIRD CLASS ORDINARY SINGLE |

PLEASE NOTIFY GUARD BEFORE BOARDING TRAIN

| Adult | Child | Special Child | Special Sen Cit | Dog Bike | Member | Camp | TOTAL FARE £ 11·60 |

Train # 1510   Date 09/06/95   Last Return Train 1610

B113558   2 B INT

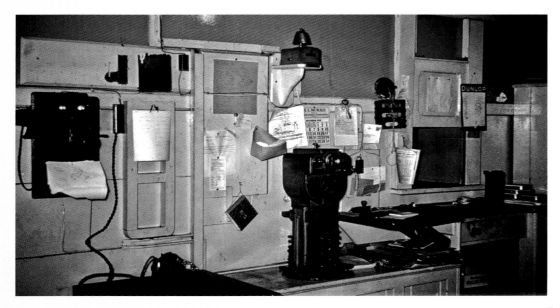

Below **PORTHMADOG:** 1963 saw the centenary celebrations of the introduction of steam traction on the FR. The new steam locomotives took over the increasingly onerous task of shifting the slate wagons to and from Blaenau Ffestiniog, where previously horses had been employed to haul empty stock up the line, then to ride down in a wagon as part of the full load descending to the port. On a dull 22 May 1963, a representation of that modus operandi is displayed in Harbour station, incidentally showing how restricted the 2-foot width between the rails was for the horse. *Mike Seymour, Howard Wilson collection*

Above **PORTHMADOG:** Akin to the proverbial iceberg, what is seen by the public on the railway is but a small proportion of the massive amount of work behind the scenes. One of the sights rarely seen is the inside of the booking office, and this, like the rest of the organisation, changes over time. In 1960 the booking office at Harbour station is captured in all its seemingly ramshackle 'glory', complete with token machine, shortly before alteration and updating. *Norman Pearce, Howard Wilson collection*

Right **PORTHMADOG:** With 'K1' restored to 'main-line' condition in the 21st century and operating on the rebuilt WHR, it could be easy to overlook the sheer volume of work and effort that has gone into its restoration and how close the loco came to actually being either scrapped or exported to the USA. The full story of this, the world's first 'Garratt' locomotive, is told elsewhere, but it is with great pride that the FR, through the WHR, is able to operate both the first and the last Garratts to be built by Beyer Peacock in Manchester. Nearly 40 years out of service but looking in reasonable condition, 'K1' stands on display in Harbour station in April 1966. It would be almost another 40 before it steamed again! *Peter Arnold*

Left **PORTHMADOG:** In 1962/3 the railway purchased two ex-Hunslet Engine Co 0-4-0STs from the Penrhyn Quarry Railway. Affectionately known as 'the Ladies' over the years, *Linda* and *Blanche* immediately gave the FR a boost in motive power strength and have been stalwarts ever since, loved by staff, volunteers and public alike. *Blanche* was reconfigured in 1972 to 2-4-0ST, with the addition of a leading pony truck utilising a wheelset from *Moel Tryfan*, a single Fairlie loco from the original WHR. A year earlier, in June 1971, she is still with original wheel arrangement as she gently reverses four 'bug boxes' onto carriage 22 at the head of a train bound for Dduallt. Note the extra carriage sidings being installed in the foreground. *Norman Pearce, Howard Wilson collection*

Below **PORTHMADOG:** Over the past two decades the FR has celebrated many successful Galas, with a variety of themes. Perhaps one of the most unusual was the 'Quirks & Curiosities' event over the Bank Holiday weekend of Saturday-Monday 1-3 May 2010, when several 'weird and wonderful' engines and contraptions paraded and were allowed to strut their stuff. In glorious weather, at precisely 1253 on 2 May, this unusual trio makes its stately way across the Cob towards Porthmadog, consisting of, right to left, vertical-boilered *Perseverance* from the Launceston Steam Railway, 0-4-0 vertical-boilered *Paddy* from the Amerton Railway and, transporting the passengers, replica Penrhyn Quarry Railway 'Car S' from the Hayfield & Whaley Bridge Light Railway. *MJS*

Overleaf **PORTHMADOG:** Another view of the Cob (to the right) from across the estuary on 29 April 2005, high up behind Boston Lodge Works. With the high tide lapping at the foot of the embankment, the more modern double-engine *Earl of Merioneth,* constructed by the railway in 1979, leaves the confines of Harbour station as the 1240 departure for Blaenau Ffestiniog. The town of Porthmadog is spread out beyond, with a much foreshortened view amply demonstrating how much is crammed into the relatively narrow available land space. The rebuilt WHR now approaches Harbour station over Britannia Bridge. *MJS*

Above **PORTHMADOG:** One of the distinctive features of the FR is the near-mile-long Cob, the embankment initiated by William Maddocks MP in the early years of the 19th century, slicing arrow-like straight across the Glaslyn estuary and cutting off the inland valley from the sea. This both provided thousands of acres of new land and created a channel, which he developed into his new harbour, ready for the slate to be received from the quarries in and around Blaenau Ffestiniog. The sea is to the right as *David Lloyd George* and *Mountaineer* approach their destination with the 1515 departure from Blaenau on 1 May 2004. The small headboard advertises the railway's presence at the NRM's 'Railfest' celebrations in York. *MJS*

BOSTON LODGE

BOSTON LODGE: Also on 2 May 2010, *Merddin Emrys* is viewed from the rear of Glan y Mor yard at Boston Lodge, heading across the Cob and about to pass the site of the short-lived Pen Cob Halt, with the nine-coach 'A Set' forming the 1210 Porthmadog-Blaenau Ffestiniog service. The distinctive hills across the valley, behind Tremadog, provide a delightful backdrop. *MJS*

Left **BOSTON LODGE:** There have been a number of liveries tried on the FR locos over the last five and a half decades, but in your author's humble opinion one of the most pleasing has been the green coat with black and red lining, as seen applied to *Taliesin*, temporarily cold and out of service in the works yard. Opened in 1806, in conjunction with the planned construction of the Cob from the following year, Boston Lodge is now the oldest surviving railway works in the world, with many of its original buildings still in use. It is also the only locomotive works anywhere to have built steam engines in the 19th, 20th and 21st centuries! *Norman Pearce, Howard Wilson collection*

Right **BOSTON LODGE:** As well as running passenger services, the railway has to maintain its surrounding and supporting infrastructure. Due to the very narrow nature of the corridor through the hilly and woody terrain along the route, opportunities to transport necessary materials by road are severely limited, leading to trains of sometimes specialised vehicles being required. In July 1963 the S&T group prepare to leave Boston Lodge with their concrete train, hauled by *Mary Ann* with an eclectic mix of Ffestiniog, Croesor tramway and industrial stock, despite the Heath Robinson appearance! *Norman Pearce, Howard Wilson collection*

Right **BOSTON LODGE:** The old entrance to the works yard used to be flanked by two large stone pillars. The one previously to the right of *Prince*, undertaking shunting duties on 6 September 1958, was demolished the year before, whereas the one between the two locos lasted until the 1980s, when it came down on safety grounds, after clearance proved inadequate for some of the crews as their engines entered the yard. Double-Fairlie *Taliesin* leans into the curve past the yard on the approach to the Cob, with its down four-coach morning train from Tan y Bwlch. When preservationists took over in 1954, much of this railway scene was under a blanket of sand, blown in from the sea over the eight years since closure in 1946. The view was to remain virtually unchanged into the 1980s. *MJS collection*

Left **BOSTON LODGE:** All private railways have items of rolling stock and motive power in store at various locations, awaiting their turn for attention and, hopefully, full restoration. The picture in Glan y Mor yard at Boston Lodge in 1962, however, does not look overly promising, despite the attempt at protection from sea, salt and sand. George England engines *Princess, Welsh Pony* and *Palmerston* almost seem abandoned amongst the greenery, but all would be moved to alternative locations, with the last-named finally restored again to full health, despite being in by far the worst condition of the three. In 2010 thoughts turned to the possibility of also adding *Welsh Pony* to the operational fleet. *Norman Pearce, Howard Wilson collection*

Above **BOSTON LODGE:** ...and here we have *Palmerston,* now very much the live animal, standing in the works yard on 6 May 1995, on the site of the demolished long shed, in company with *Sgt Murphy* and *Upnor Castle,* during another Mayday Bank Holiday weekend. *Sgt Murphy's* owner and FR General Manager at the time, Gordon Rushton, casually chats in 'hands on' working mode, hands in pockets and complete with braces and cap, during the morning's preparatory business. The impressive Porthmadog backdrop of Moel y Gest looms in the distance. *MJS*

Left **BOSTON LODGE:** The origins of Boston Lodge Works and its heritage have already been recorded and here we have a peep inside the ancient building. In 1972, during the 'close season', *Blanche* is on the immediate left, with 'sister' *Linda* far right and the new double-Fairlie *Earl of Merioneth* at an early stage of construction far left. All manner of tasks are under way, with chains and hooks for lifting at the ready and sundry requisite materials to hand. *Norman Kneale, MJS collection*

Below **BOSTON LODGE:** *Merddin Emrys* has worn a number of coats in his 130 years of service to the FR and one would probably say that black does not suit him as well as some other colours, but in this portrait of a temporary ex-works coat, on the sunny early afternoon of 29 April 2005, enhanced by the low angle, the effect is very pleasing. The oldest operating double-Fairlie on the railway and named after a 6th-century Welsh poet, he was still oil-fired at this point, but would be converted to coal-firing during the winter of 2006/7. The proximity and steepness of the hill behind the works is well exemplified here. *MJS*

Above **BOSTON LODGE:** Outside again, the fourth surviving England engine, No 2 *Prince*, stands resplendent in his bright red coat on 29 July 1991, totally belying his age of 128 years! To his right is the new order, the 1958-vintage, ex-Admiralty 'Planet' diesel *Conway Castle/Castell Conwy*, brought to the railway in 1981. The building behind, self-evidently of newer vintage than the adjacent structure, was completed in the mid-1960s and acts as an extension to the former carriage shed. Together they have formed the locomotive running shed, but it is now cramped and life-expired and it is proposed to replace it with a more modern facility. *MJS*

Right **BOSTON LODGE:** Smoke and steam abound as the 'old' *Earl of Merioneth* storms away from a brief stop at Boston Lodge Halt on 25 April 1970. The old weigh house, since in use for various purposes, and the attached engine shed stand alongside the single track, beyond the coaches. (The red line is on the original slide, but such dramatic steam could not be resisted!) *Peter Arnold*

BOSTON LODGE: Another exhibition of pyrotechnics, but this time a little more under control. The fireman of *Palmerston* leans from the cab to monitor the photographer's position as the train pulls out all the stops to regain momentum after a stop at the Halt on Sunday 2 May 2010, at the head of the 1147 Porthmadog Harbour-Tan-y-Bwlch train, during the 'Quirks & Curiosities' weekend. Note how the lineside to the left has been tidied. *MJS*

Left **BOSTON LODGE:** Turning to look north, the 'old' *Earl of Merioneth* is seen again, this time around 1962, arriving at the Halt with a down train from Tan y Bwlch. Less than a decade into preservation, the railway has progressively extended northwards, with incidentals such as fencing not necessarily taking top priority, but the loco and coaching stock have all received appropriate coats of paint. A good supply of coal sits on top of the tank. An Austin A40 Devon, possibly from around 1950/51, stands to the left. *Peter Arnold*

LOTTIE'S COTTAGE

Left **LOTTIE'S COTTAGE:** The climb up from sea level begins in earnest at Boston Lodge and does not let up for the next dozen miles or so. Roughly three-quarters of a mile north of the Lodge, *Prince* and *Blanche* double-head an unusually long mixed train on 1 August 1966, passing a reminder of the past in the form of a disc signal and approaching the road crossing by Lottie's Cottage. A Grade 2 listed building, the cottage was the crossing keeper's house, and the late Mrs Lottie Edwards was the last incumbent. She was ever kind and helpful to the railway, and the FR has renovated the building in her memory. *Peter Arnold*

MINFFORDD

MINFFORDD: We have made mention previously of the worth of volunteers to the railway. It is often hard, back-breaking work and largely unsung by the general public, but, quite simply, without their involvement we would not have the wonderful railway that countless thousands enjoy every year.

In earlier times, shirt sleeves are rolled up in the spring of 1965 for the effort of offloading spoil to create a more solid base for a second siding. Note the ex-RAF wagons, acquired second-hand in the 1960s, around a decade old at the time. They have done half a century of stalwart service since then! *Roy Wakeford*

Right **MINFFORDD:** Closely Observed Train! We are now approaching Minffordd station and are standing on the foot crossing into the goods yard. 'Farmer Giles' takes a breather from his duties to watch the passage of a down train. On 6 May 1995 double-Fairlie *David Lloyd George* is not working hard downhill, but equally is not in great shape as it leaves Minffordd station with the 1615 Blaenau Ffestiniog-Porthmadog service, the bottom-end fire being out! MJS

FFESTINIOG
STEAM 125
1863-1988

3018

Ffestiniog Railway

WEEKEND ROVER TICKET

Valid 30th April - 2nd May 1988
on ALL regular trains between

Porthmadog
AND
BLAENAU FFESTINIOG

NOT TRANSFERABLE   Issued
subject to the Company's Bye-Laws &
Conditions. *For full validity* SEE BACK

FFESTINIOG RAILWAY

3018

WELSH HIGHLAND RAILWAY

Valid for travel on the

W.H.R.

30 APRIL - 2 MAY 1988

Above **MINFFORDD:** Closer to the station – seen in the background – another double engine heads south for Porthmadog. On AGM day, 27 April 1968, the 'old' *Earl of Merioneth,* complete with Observation Car 100 immediately behind, restarts from the Minffordd stop and heads for its destination at Harbour station. The driver takes a brief moment to share some pleasantry with a lineside onlooker. The roof of a passing car can be seen on the A487 road to the right. *Peter Arnold*

Right **MINFFORDD:** Over the passage of five and half decades since the restorationists took over, the railway has found time and resources to attend to the finer things of making the experience more pleasing and enjoyable for the visitor. With the trackbed and surroundings looking very neat and tidy, *Prince* and *Blanche* haul a long rake northwards into the station on 23 August 2009, operating as the 1015 Porthmadog-Blaenau Ffestiniog morning train. Note the narrow foot crossing at the platform ends and the provision of both colour lights and a replica disc signal, here with its stop face clearly showing to down traffic. *MJS*

Below **MINFFORDD:** A delight for onlookers and, indeed, for those riding the rather uncomfortable mode of transport, the railway enjoys recreating a downward run by a gravity train. Utilising the constant down gradient over the line, a long rake of slate-filled wagons gliding 'silently' downhill with only 'brakesmen' atop the slates to control them, fills spectators with joy and amazement in equal share. By the 21st century the FR was the possessor of an impressive rake, but the very first such demonstration, on 22 May 1963, has just four wagons, and is seen running through Minffordd station loop. *Mike Seymour, Howard Wilson collection*

MINFFORDD: A third view of a double-Fairlie heading south has *Merddin Emrys* in the station, temporarily at rest and blowing off with steam to spare, on a sunny afternoon in July 1973, while en route between Dduallt and Porthmadog. Note again the attractive green coat with black and red lining, the prominent brass dome, the pseudo-gas lamp on the station wall, and the rake of coaches, including the Observation Car No 100, now in red livery, compared to the earlier shot in 1968. *Norman Pearce, Howard Wilson collection*

GWYNDY BANK

GWYNDY BANK: Yet another look at the Observation Car and yet another outer incarnation. With the green and yellow stock behind it, *Linda* runs tender-first down Gwyndy Bank on 1 August 1966, over the slate embankment and bridge, largely untouched since its creation 130 years earlier! Note the photographer's 1964-vintage Prussian Blue Vauxhall Viva HA parked on the narrow grass verge and the tight and blind turn from the side road to go under the bridge. With her open cab, travelling tender-first is a draughty experience at the best of times for *Linda's* crew! *Peter Arnold*

GWYNDY BANK: Like Topsy, the FR's gravity train rake of wagons has continued to grow with provision now available for a truly lengthy and memorable experience. Considerably longer than the mere four cars seen at Minffordd, this set is at least twice that size as it rattles past the Claytons' front room on 2 May 2004, with a great many more brakesmen on hand to prevent mayhem. The longest rake recorded in preservation had 39 wagons – a long way to go to match the 100-wagon trains of the old company! *MJS*

TY FRY CURVE

TY FRY CURVE: Around a quarter of a mile north of Gwyndy, the track negotiates a roughly 45° right-hand curve going up the line and, judging by the Vauxhall Viva at the end of the lane, the photographer has transported himself from the Bank to capture *Prince* on another working with the same stock as seen coupled to *Linda*. The date is again 1 August 1966 and the train, from Tan y Bwlch, is about to unwind from the radius of the curve. The fireman appears to be enjoying a brief respite from his labours in the opening to the tender. *Peter Arnold*

TY FRY CURVE: The same photographer, but a different day, and the same location, but now looking south. Back with the varnished teak livery in use at that time, *Linda,* still in her 0-4-0ST form, heads north on 25 April 1970 with a Porthmadog-Dduallt service, entering the curve on the climb from Gwyndy. The young lads in the leading coach are obviously transfixed at the opportunity to witness the journey from their vantage point. *Peter Arnold*

Above **PENRHYNDEUDRAETH:** Two more youngsters seem awe-struck on 1 August 1966 and, perhaps, a little unsure as *Prince*, adorned with a star on the smokebox, makes the final few yards of the climb into the station confines with its train for Tan y Bwlch. Note the pointwork for the turnout to the loop in the station. *Peter Arnold*

Right **PENRHYNDEUDRAETH:** The trackwork in the station has undergone various shifts in thought and traffic needs, the latest configuration being just a single line through the station. On Friday, 13 July 1973, however, the loop line – installed in 1957 and lengthened in 1969 – is still in place, as the line only extends as far as Dduallt and this passing place was required for timetable stability. *Linda* enters with her train for the temporary northern outpost at Dduallt, as a downward one waits for the token for the single track southwards. A passing loop was installed a little over half a mile north at Rhiw Goch in 1975, so Penrhyn loop ceased to be used from the end of 1974 and was subsequently removed. *Horace Gamble, MJS collection*

Above **PENRHYNDEUDRAETH:** With all the attention from photographers, one could almost say 'cheese' to *Linda* as she leaves the station and prepares to cross the A4085 Beddgelert road on her journey north. In heady days before the current obsession with Health & Safety, her progress towards Tan y Bwlch in April 1968, with mixed coaching stock, is witnessed inside the closed crossing gates. Note the very wise 'No Parking' sign outside the houses, and the proliferation of television aerials. *Dennis Weaver, MJS collection*

Right **PENRHYNDEUDRAETH:** By 7 June 2003 most of the houses have upgraded to indoor TV aerials, judging by the chimney tops, as *Taliesin* leaves the road crossing and heads north with another Porthmadog-Blaenau Ffestiniog train. The headboard marks the celebration of 140 years of steam on the railway. Self-built by the FR at Boston Lodge Works, the loco was new in 1999, recreating an earlier incarnation that had emerged from Vulcan Foundry in 1876. Parts of the original loco, which was scrapped in 1935, were used in the new one, which has the status of being the sole single-Fairlie on the line and the only working example in the world. *MJS*

PENRHYNDEUDRAETH: Standing by the crossing gates, we now look up the line as *Linda* accelerates away from the station stop in June 1971 with a train bound for Dduallt. This once open aspect is now hidden behind many years of arboreal growth, concealing from view the white house, top left, in which supporters of and volunteers on the railway have lived for many years. Note the photographer up a ladder against the telegraph pole beyond the second carriage! *Norman Pearce, Howard Wilson collection*

PEN CEFN

Left **PEN CEFN:** Just yards beyond the last view, the 'old' *Earl of Merioneth* heads down the gradient on 7 August 1967, hemmed between the stone boundary walls, with the 3.45pm train from Tan y Bwlch. The driver takes a casual look ahead, to ensure that the way is clear for his approach to the road crossing and that the gates will be set for rail and not road. *Peter Arnold*

Below **Near RHIW GOCH:** The increasingly wilderness nature of the surrounding terrain as the line travels north is well displayed in this view of *Blanche* descending with a train from Tan y Bwlch on 15 April 1968. It is clear how the railway has to make constant zigzags as it negotiates its path along the hillside, and it is still impressive to consider both that the railway overcame the doubters to successfully create a railway through the landscape on such a narrow gauge, and that it was constructed on a continually falling gradient down to sea level! *Peter Arnold*

Below **RHIW GOCH:** A little over 4 miles from Harbour station, the passing loop here was opened on 14 May 1975, enabling that previously in place at Penrhyndeudraeth to be abandoned. It has seen changes in 'fashion' as the railway has progressed ever further northwards to Blaenau Ffestiniog, but such has been the consequent explosion in visitor numbers that the signal box here has been regularly manned since the 2005 season. As a down train waits for its path behind the photographer, *David Lloyd George* heads up the line on 1 May 2005 with the 1020 Porthmadog-Blaenau Ffestiniog service. *MJS*

WHISTLING CURVE

Right **WHISTLING CURVE:** We have already seen *Merddin Emrys* in this condition in Harbour station, but the loco is here out on the line with an open wagon, 1918-vintage diesel *Moelwyn* and a handful of sparsely occupied carriages, climbing towards Tan y Bwlch in 1962. Just over 2½ miles north of Rhiw Goch, the curve is so named as trains do indeed whistle here, to alert staff at Tan y Bwlch, across the valley, that the service is approaching. *Norman Pearce, Howard Wilson collection*

Opposite bottom **MILEPOST 7:** Just yards further on, 'old' *Earl of Merioneth* passes this location on 6 August 1962, with the 1030 train from Porthmadog to Tan y Bwlch. A wagon full of materials is part of the consist and this could well have been in connection with the major work being undertaken further north. *Peter Arnold*

Above **MILEPOST 7:** Close to the same point, but now viewed from above, *Prince* rounds the curve and trundles its way north towards Tan y Bwlch with a load of seven of the small coaches in April 1966. Sadly, so many of these sorts of views have become unavailable over recent years as the trees and undergrowth have pursued their relentless growth. Although recent forestry cutting back has improved the situation, it is still nowhere near as clear as seen here. *Peter Arnold*

Left **TAN Y BWLCH:** To many, North Wales is synonymous with rain and, yes, it does occasionally pour! In the midst of just such a storm, on 9 April 2004, *Linda*, now as a 2-4-0ST, climbs the last few yards into the station, with both crew members intent on what lies ahead. She is here at the head of one of the FR's short-lived 'Talking Trains', an innovation whereby participants could listen to handsets explaining the surrounding highlights as the train passed certain strategic points, denoted by numbered plaques. *MJS*

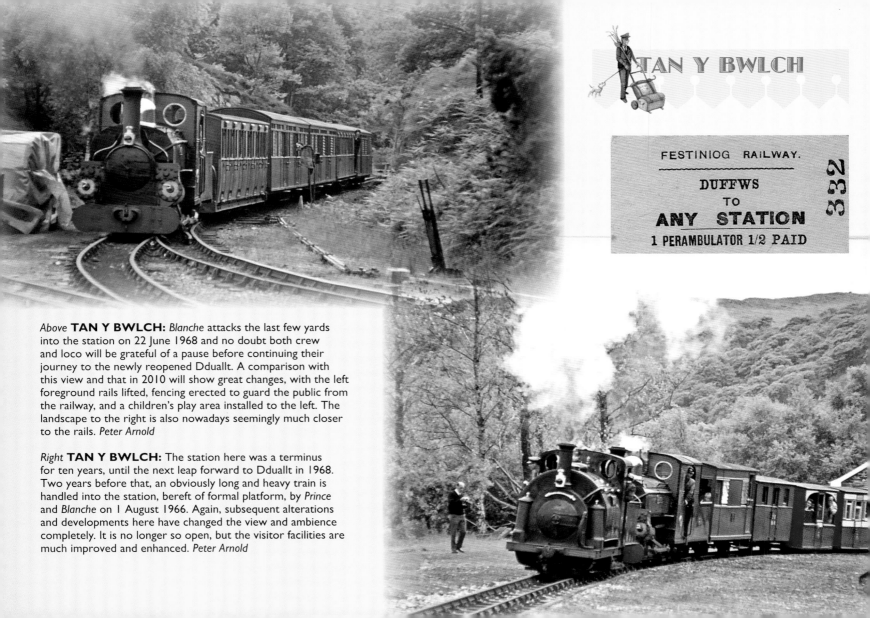

FESTINIOG RAILWAY.

DUFFWS
TO
ANY STATION

1 PERAMBULATOR 1/2 PAID

332

Above **TAN Y BWLCH:** *Blanche* attacks the last few yards into the station on 22 June 1968 and no doubt both crew and loco will be grateful of a pause before continuing their journey to the newly reopened Dduallt. A comparison with this view and that in 2010 will show great changes, with the left foreground rails lifted, fencing erected to guard the public from the railway, and a children's play area installed to the left. The landscape to the right is also nowadays seemingly much closer to the rails. *Peter Arnold*

Right **TAN Y BWLCH:** The station here was a terminus for ten years, until the next leap forward to Dduallt in 1968. Two years before that, an obviously long and heavy train is handled into the station, bereft of formal platform, by *Prince* and *Blanche* on 1 August 1966. Again, subsequent alterations and developments here have changed the view and ambience completely. It is no longer so open, but the visitor facilities are much improved and enhanced. *Peter Arnold*

TAN Y BWLCH: Once more, volunteers to the rescue! Long before the development of a more formal youth recruitment policy, led by Eileen Clayton with the Parks & Gardens department, a young team is deep in concentration on the ground, under the tutelage of Norman Gurley, who was a long-term servant of the railway and became one of its finest and most prolific photographers. Note the wide open space in the background, with just one car, as the re-sleepering work is undertaken during Easter 1966. *Howard Wilson*

TAN Y BWLCH: Another 'behind the scenes' view. The date is 1968 and Dduallt has opened. A works train of (mostly) filled ballast wagons stands behind *Prince,* which looks in remarkably good condition. It will not be long before the platform is created here, begun on 20 May that year. *Norman Pearce, Howard Wilson collection*

Right **TAN Y BWLCH:** There are not many colour photographs of the travelling public on the FR in the late-Victorian era … and, yes, this is not one of them! As part of the centenary celebrations on 22 May 1963, a collection of the 'good and wealthy' alight from a genuine vintage train and proceed towards the top end of the station. A number of local people were invited to travel in Victorian costume and all are upright and properly dressed – no T-shirts, trainers, baseball caps or slouching here! The guard is Ross Gregory – complete with artificial beard! *Mike Seymour, Howard Wilson collection*

Left **TAN Y BWLCH:** Coming much more up-to-date, *Palmerston* stands 'wrong road' in the station on 26 October 1996 during a 'Vintage Weekend' mini-gala, having brought its passengers up the line as the 1145 'Flying Flea' set from Porthmadog. For many years the FR has defied convention by passing on the right, rather than keeping to the left as on other railways and on the roads. *MJS*

FESTINIOG RY. | FESTINIOG RY.
RETURN HALF | Notice.- This Ticket is
Notice,- This Ticket is | issued subject to the
issued subject to the | conditions on the Time
conditions on the Time | Tables of the Company
Tables of the Company |
BLAENAU | Tany Bwlch
FESTINIOG JUNC TO | TO BLAENAU
TANY BWLCH, | FESTINIOG JUNC.
First Class 2/2 | First Class 2/2

Below **TAN Y BWLCH:** The oldest colour slide in this collection portrays *Taliesin* at the water tank on 16 April 1960. A lady appears to be taking the opportunity of experiencing the narrow confines of this side of the loco's cab. Note the very open and uncluttered backdrop and the simple track layout. Only re-opened in 1958, the station was beginning to build its reputation as a place to visit, with Llyn Mair and many country walks nearby. *J E Arnold, Peter Arnold collection*

Inset right **TAN Y BWLCH:** The water tank is again seen, this time with many more people in attendance. In May 1964, *Prince* receives refreshment, while its passengers come forward for a view of the operation before either enjoying the ride back to Porthmadog or, alternatively, going for a walk and taking

a later train down the line. Judging by the apparel, the weather was being none too kind! *J K Morton, MJS collection*

Right **GARNEDD TUNNEL:** The aforementioned Llyn Mair is below to the left as the railway makes its way north from Tan y Bwlch along the very narrow ledge on the hillside. This angle, on an unidentified date, superbly demonstrates how clever were the builders of the route, defying scepticism and, at times, gravity! Moelwyn emerges from the tunnel on the current alignment, towing the weedkiller wagon, clearly needed in this pre-1968 re-opening shot. Amazing to think that the railway initially ran around this tunnel outcrop on the even narrower ledge to the left! *Roy Wakeford*

GARNEDD TUNNEL: The northern approach to the tunnel gives one of the most stunning views across the Afon Dwyryd valley. The three lineside workers in the background have no doubt cast their eyes in that direction at times, but here are concentrating on being out of the way of the six-coach train as it rounds the curve heading south. On 15 April 1968, nine days after Dduallt returned to the timetable, the 'old' *Earl of Merioneth* is again seen earning its keep as it operates one of the earliest trains from the newly opened station. *Peter Arnold*

Right **COED Y BLEDDIAU:** The FR is famous in part for its fabulous historical context within the UK's overall railway narrative, but it is also infamous for a reason that is not widely known. The cottage sited midway between Garnedd Tunnel and Campbell's Platform has the name Coed y Bleddiau, which means 'Wood of the Wolves', and this is strangely prophetic and appropriate in that a one-time occupant was one William Joyce, aka 'Lord Haw Haw', who broadcast propaganda from Nazi Germany during the Second World War in the programme *Germany Calling*. He was hanged for treason on 3 January 1946. In calmer times, a group of volunteers, including Major Charles Walker in the foreground, here set about repairing telegraph communications in July 1965, with the cottage, situated miles from anywhere, seen through the trees. *Norman Pearce, Howard Wilson collection*

Left **CAMPBELL'S PLATFORM:** Set above Dduallt Manor, Campbell's Platform was established for the benefit of Colonel Campbell, the owner of the Manor and possessor of a gunpowder licence, which contributed mightily, in all senses, to the creation of the spiral around Dduallt station. The 'Deviationists' who created what we see today were also to use the Halt as they enjoyed mess facilities for a time in one of his barns. Situated adjacent to milepost 9, *Linda* is alongside the short platform on 1 September 1968 as she tackles the climb towards the temporary terminus at Dduallt, with the Colonel's simplex loco in the siding. As a matter of interest – and continuing the rebellion theme – this was Cromwell's North Wales HQ during the Civil War! *Peter Arnold*

Above **CAMPBELL'S PLATFORM:** On the ground on 3 May 2004, the sweeping 'Tank Curve', on the southern approach to the location, is wide open to view, and very noticeable is the effect of landscaping of the site, with the siding dispensed with, grass sown, a flower bed in place, and a seat on which to watch the trains pass by and while away the quiet moments in between. A tiny waiting shelter stands on the left. *MJS*

Above **DDUALLT:** Between trains, this location is another haven of peace, being almost a Welsh equivalent of the American badlands, miles from any road and/or habitation, with rugged countryside only inhabited by nature and the occasional sheep. The railway can seem apologetic as it cuts through the topography. On 25 May 1969 the 'old' *Earl of Merioneth* is seen once more, beginning its journey back to Porthmadog, with the station, then the temporary terminus, behind. That work is still in progress in forging the next stretch north can be judged by the skeleton of a new facility to first shift rock from Barn cutting, then take the new track over the lower level. Note that this new erection is much higher than the earlier footbridge, as the new railway will need to climb onto a brand new trajectory. *Peter Arnold*

Left **DDUALLT:** The station opened in 1968 as the northern terminus while work continued to build the line further towards Blaenau Ffestiniog. In August of that year, passengers can spend their time walking the hill while the train engine runs round, but it is obvious that much work is still to be done to make the station presentable. The 'old' *Earl of Merioneth* uses the loop to run round its train, which will then have the Observation Car immediately behind the engine, before retracing the route south. *Norman Pearce, Howard Wilson collection*

Above right **DDUALLT:** Further evidence that work is still in hand in connection with opening the station is clear from the fresh ballast under the train and the naked scar caused by the run-round loop on the right. In 1968 the 'old' *Earl of Merioneth* is again in charge, in its delightful green lined livery, having run round its train prior to departure. To the left, before the First World War, Rhossllyn House was the home of 'station master' Gwilym Deudraeth, a Welsh bard who wrote of the depressing effect of such a lonely place. However, on a warm sunny day it is now an ideal place to bring a picnic lunch, alighting from an up train and reboarding it as it returns south. *Dennis Weaver, MJS collection*

ARCHER DAM

Opposite bottom left **DDUALLT:** By 3 May 2004 the place looks decidedly more civilised, with a proper platform, a running-in sign and even the house having had a coat of whitewash at some time in the past. The background is much as before, but the telegraph pole has been enhanced, the house windows have been opened then reboarded, the stone pillar outside the house fencing has shrunk, and the tree on the left has grown. Painted in former Penrhyn Quarry livery, *Linda* arrives with the 1315 Blaenau Ffestiniog-Porthmadog train. *MJS*

Below **TUNNEL NORTH CUTTING:** The original route north from Dduallt ran through the 730-yard Moelwyn Tunnel, gouged through the southern flank of the eponymous mountain range in 1842. The flooding of this route north of that tunnel by a reservoir dictated that the FR find another

route, hence the 'deviation' at Dduallt and the climb to higher ground. This still meant a tunnel, but of shorter length – just 287 yards – and this was finally opened on 24 June 1977, when *Merddin Emrys*, with the appropriate headboard of 'Blaenau Ffestiniog here we come!', blasts from the northern portal of the new tunnel in explosive fashion on its way to Llyn Ystradau. The original route at Tanygrisiau station was regained the following year, and Blaenau Ffestiniog was reached in 1982. *MJS collection*

Above right **ARCHER DAM:** Forging onwards from the tunnel, the next obstacle was a wall of the 1836 Archer Dam, named after the railway's original investor. It drove a waterwheel, which hauled loaded slate trains up an incline over the Moelwyn spur until the tunnel was completed in 1842; it had to be breached for the railway to progress further beyond the new tunnel. The 'hole' through the wall is seen in July 1974, with the temporary track installed to transport rock from cutting faces to embankment heads. Some of the skip wagons can be seen in front of and next to the metal box. In the distance, the 'scar' shows the proposed route ahead. *Norman Pearce, Howard Wilson collection*

Right **ARCHER DAM:** The railway continued its inexorable progress onwards and the line through the dam opened to the public in 1977, at another temporary terminus named

Llyn Ystradau, alongside the flooded valley. That short-lived Halt was to the right beyond the end of the train. In a patch of sunlight *Prince* and *Conway Castle* make their way south on 2 May 1993 with the 1300 Blaenau Ffestiniog-Porthmadog train, here running some 40 minutes late. The height of the surrounding hillsides is obvious from this view, encouraging the lineside photographers. *MJS*

Above **LLYN YSTRADAU:** The temporary terminal platform here lasted for just a year, from 1977 until 1978, when the next stage to Tanygrisiau was opened. The location was just behind the final carriage in this 11-coach rake forming the 1150 Blaenau Ffestiniog-Porthmadog train on 3 May 2004, being taken back south behind the 'new' *Earl of Merioneth,* completed in 1979. The pathway to the right of the train is the old 1836 trackbed that led to the tunnel that was flooded by the reservoir. The power station for this can be seen behind the train. *MJS*

Below **LLYN YSTRADAU:** We are now closer to the CEGB power station, built over the old trackbed, and the reason for the spiral to climb up the hillside at Dduallt, to create a route north, is clear to see. Preparations for the next extension, to Tanygrisiau, are ahead and to the left in January 1978, with the Llyn Ystradau platform behind the camera; the new track has its sleepers in place but is not yet ballasted. A measuring wheel is being employed as others photograph the work in progress. *Norman Pearce, Howard Wilson collection*

miles from Harbour, *Prince* is probably relieved to make this destination on 12 July 1980, welcomed by enthusiasts and intending passengers. Again the backdrop is awesome. *MJS*

Below **TANYGRISIAU:** The layout at the station has changed over the years, and after opening to Blaenau Ffestiniog the loop was removed, as seen here as *Linda* leads *Blanche* out of the station on 2 May 1993, running 40 minutes late as the 1200 service to Porthmadog. The platform is also receiving some attention, with the far end being truncated. Note that the white house, behind, has had extensions over the intervening 13 years. *MJS*

Previous page **TANYGRISIAU:** Once again we can see the magnitude of the backdrop in this upper part of the railway, as *David Lloyd George* approaches Tanygrisiau station on 18 April 1998, double-heading with Funkey diesel *Vale of Ffestiniog*, which was to be put on display at Blaenau Ffestiniog station (see later). The train is running on the new track, beyond the old house, with the 1836 trackbed, now the approach road to the pumping station, in front of it, beyond the low wall. Note that the reservoir for the pumped storage scheme is at a low level. *MJS*

Above **TANYGRISIAU:** After opening in 1978, Tanygrisiau was as far as travellers could go for the next four years, but the mere presence here showed the FR's determination to make the final goal and the visitors kept coming. Now some 12¼

Above **TANYGRISIAU:** Looking south at the station today, it is hardly conceivable that this March 1972 vista is the same location, such has been the challenge and achievement by the volunteers and others in creating the current highly serviceable station. The goods shed by the abandoned cars is still in place but, as the general ground level was some 3 feet lower, more of it was revealed then than today. In addition, the right-hand side has been drastically re-landscaped by dynamite, to shoe-horn the desired station on to a new rock shelf. *Norman Pearce, Howard Wilson collection*

Below left **TANYGRISIAU:** On 26 October 1996, during that year's Vintage Weekend and with plenty of steam available for the final lap, *Blanche* and *Mountaineer* (here alias '1265' following its appearance as a First World War loco the year before) slowly get to grips with the road away from the area created by gunpowder, with the 1350 Porthmadog-Blaenau Ffestiniog train. The rails in the foreground are in readiness for the reinstallation of the loop, to enable trains to pass here, although this was not completed for some years. *MJS*

Below **GLAN Y PWLL:** For the last few yards into Blaenau Ffestiniog the railway passes the Permanent Way Depot, with an appropriate sign regarding the railway's ambitions. Seen from the adjacent footbridge – since closed – *Linda* is the centre of attention as she crosses the local road on 25 May 1982, as the second train into the new terminus. Note the second line next to the train, for a planned extension to the quarries at Dinas that never came to pass; and the 'mountain' of slate waste in the background. *Peter Treloar, MJS collection*

BLAENAU FFESTINIOG

Right **BLAENAU FFESTINIOG:** We are almost there! From 1962, when quarry traffic ceased, until the FR regained access to the town from the south – after more than 35 years – the only track that still had traffic was the British Rail line for nuclear waste trains to and from Trawsfynydd, via a connection from the old ex-LMS station (through the bridge in the centre distance). The track in the right foreground was the remains of the original FR route, grassed over after ten years without any traffic, through Blaenau Central, the ex-GWR station (behind the camera) to Duffws, which was the former terminus for the railway and the quarries. This view is from March 1972. *Norman Pearce, Howard Wilson collection*

Left **BLAENAU FFESTINIOG:** In the same view 21 years later, the two 'Ladies' shut off after their long climb and prepare to drift into the new FR station on 2 May 1993, with the 1045 train from Porthmadog, 45 minutes late through no fault of their own! Left of the lineside is relatively little changed, but elsewhere, on the ground, in the distance and to the right, there has been dramatic alteration. Note also that the BR and FR tracks have 'swapped sides', with the end of the 1982 BR platform on the right. *MJS*

Left **BLAENAU FFESTINIOG:** Being the terminus, waiting passengers and enthusiasts have the chance to see trains on both BR and FR turning round; on the latter the loco runs round to take up position at the southern end. On 2 May 1993 *David Lloyd George* has successfully completed the task and waits to return to Porthmadog with the 1200 service, all the carriages of which are more than 100 years older than the 1990-built locomotive! The BR station is to the left, the Queen's Hotel, long a landmark in the town, stands beyond the last coach, and more slate waste dominates the horizon. *MJS*

Right **BLAENAU FFESTINIOG:** We have already seen Funkey diesel *Vale of Ffestiniog* being double-headed up the line for display on 18 April 1998, and here it is with 'big brother'! With National Power contributing to the painting of the Funkey, it was appropriate to arrange this meeting with 'The Roman Nose' railtour, headed by NP's similarly liveried Class 59 No 59205 *L. Keith McNair*. Local interest is obvious from all the sightseers present. Note the extra FR track that is now in place. *MJS*

INDEX

PORTHMADOG: Playing its part in the celebrations, Lyd shunts the stock at Harbour Station, Porthmadog, on 30 October 2010, ready for the 12.50 Porthmadog-Caernarfon return leg of the historic first ever Caernarfon-Porthmadog passenger train. *MJS*